T0142697

WORDS CHOOSE WISELY

DES MOTS choisis sagement
PALABRAS eligelas sabiamente

PAOLA IGLESIAS

Balboa Press books may be ordered through booksellers or by contacting:

Balboa Press
A Division of Hay House
1663 Liberty Drive
Bloomington, IN 47403
www.balboapress.com.au
1 (877) 407-4847

Interior Graphics/Art Credit: Oscar McLeod

ISBN: 978-1-5043-2211-9 (sc)
ISBN: 978-1-5043-2212-6 (e)

Print information available on the last page.

Balboa Press rev. date: 08/17/2020

To all of us that use words choose wisely

Pour tous le monde que utilise des mot choisis sagement

Para todos nosotros que usamos palabras hay que elegirlas sabiamente.

We are all the same we are human, whether we have gone to school or not, whether we have money or don't, whether we live in big house or have no house at all. What we all have in common is LANGUAGE,there are 6500 languages spoken in the world - imagine how many WORDS!!
We just have three languages on this page spoken in many countries. WORDS we must choose wisely

Nous sommes tous le meme, nous sommes humain. Peut être que nous sommes allé a l'école, ou pas . Peut être que nous sommes riches ou non. Peut être que nous avon une maison très grand ou pas de maison. Ce que nous avons en comune c'est le langage.
Il y a 6500 langages dans toute la tierre entier . Imaginez tout les Mots!!!
Il y a seulement trois langage dans c'est page. Mots - il faut le choisir sagement

Somos todos iguales, somos humanos. Si fuimos al colegio o no. Si tenemos dinero o no si vivimos en una casa grande o quizá ni siquiera tenemos una casa. Lo que todos tenemos en común es un idioma, en le mundo hay 6500 idiomas- imagínate cuantas Palabras.
Solo tenemos tres idiomas en esta pagina- Palabras hah que elegirlas sabiamente.

Words are important. Important to you and to others . Choose wisely. The world we live in, the communities we live in are so diverse.

Look around you now how many people from different places do you see? So many people speaking different languages,though the words they choose to use have the same impact no matter where you come from or who they are.

Les mots sont important Important pour vous et des autres. Choisi sagement. Le monde dans nous habitons c'est très diverse.

Regarde autour des tois, combien des personnes de different endroits voyez-vous? Donc le gens parlent différent langues. Bien que les mots qu'il choisissent aient le meme impact n'import d'out vous venez ou qu'ils sont.

Palabras son importantes. Importantes para ti y para los demás. Eligelas sabiamente. El mundo en el que vivimos, y nuestras comunidades son tan diversas.

Mira a tu alrededor cuanta gente de lugers different ves. Tanta genet que hable idiomas diferentes pero el uso de sus palabras son iguales . no importa en que idioma tiene el mismo efecto.

We all use an alphabet one letter can mean so much ....

El alfabeto todos usamos el alfabeto una letra puede tener tanto sentido.......

L'alphabet, seulement une lettre peut dire beacoup......

A   E   I   O   U

E   Y   O   I

Look at the power of two letters in making words with meanings no matter what language

Regardez le pouvoir de deux lettres n'importer pas quelle langue

El poder de dos letras juntas para crear palabras no importa en que idioma los idiomas

AM	IN	ON	OR	NO
ES	ET	IL	OU	SI
SI	NO	EL		

The interesting thing about language is that we put words together to make sentences and give us meanings.

La chose interesant de la langue ce que mots combine formais de phrases

Lo interesante de los idiomas es que podemos unir palabras para hacer una frase que tiene sentido para nosotros

I am.......

Yo soy...

Je suis...

You are...

Tu eres...

Tu es...

The next word you choose is the most important . Which word would you choose today for you? Which word would you choose to say to others?

Quels mots choisirez vous pour vous-memes aujourd'hui et pour toi et pour autres?

Que palabra vas a elegir hoy para ti y para describir a otros?

I am, you are, he is, she is ....
happy, sad, smart, clever,angry,
silly,dumb, pretty, ugly,beautiful,
shy, dirty,

Je suis, tu es, il est, elle est .....
heureuse, triste, intelligente, habille,
stupide,debile, timide, furieux,
jolie,moche, salissant, capable

Yo soy/estoy, tu eres, el es ella es
feliz, triste, intelligente, timida,
debil, hermoso, bella, fea/
o,sucia/o, enojado/da, linda/o

So you see words are so interesting in describing how we feel about ourselves or others there are so many choices. We must choose wisely.

Comme tu peut voir il'a un plenitude des mots pour décrire comment nous nous sentons et des autres . Il faut choisir sagement

Como puedes ver la seleccion de palabras amplia para describir como nos sentimos y también como hacemos sentir a los demás. Hay que elegir sabiamente.

When you choose nice words how do they make you feel inside?
when the words you choose are not so nice how do they make you feel? Words do not leave bruises that you can see but you can certainly Feel the power of words some words have a lot of weight.

Quand tu choisis des mots gentils, comment vous sentez-vous?et si le mots ne sont pas gentiles qu'est -ce qui ce passe? Les mots ne laissent pas d'ecchymoses mais ils ont du pouvoir et du poids

Cuando eliges palabras lindas como te hacen sentir?
Y cuando eliges palabras no tan lindas que pasa? Palabras no dejan moretones per si uno puede sentír el peso de las palabras, el poder de las palabras

So imagine the impact of your words on others? Just like that words can make you into a friend or a bully? Which are you? Think about it? Which would you rather be? You have a choice.

Pouvez-vous imaginer l'impact de vos paroles sur les autres? Juste comme ca tu peut etre un ami o un intimidateur? Qui es vous? Pense y? qui veut tu être? c'est ton choix

Así que Imaginate el impacto de tus palabras en otras personas? Así nomas palabras te convierten en un amigo o en un matón. Quien eres tu? Piénsalo . Quien prefieres ser? Tu puedes elegir .

What do you gain by not being nice to others?Does it make you feel important? Does it make you feel special? How do you think the person you are saying the words to feels? You can choose your words. choose wisely

Que gagnez-vous a ne pas être gentil avec les autres? Cela vous fait-il sentir important. Cela vous fait- il sentir spécial? Comment pensez-vousque la personne se sent? Tu peut choisis tes mots. Choisis sagement.

Que logras si no tratas a alguien bien? si usas tus palabras para dañarlos ? Te hace sentir importante? Te hace sentir especial ? common piensas que la otra persona se esta sintiendo? Tu puedes elegir tus palabras . Elige sabiamente.

We learn how to treat others from our own families. Do we like how we are treated at home? Do we like how we are spoken to?How do we like to make others feel? Words are important. You cannot take words back once they are out there

Nous apprenons comment traiter les autres dents propres families. Aimons nous la façon don't nous sommes tratais a la maison ? Aimons-nous la façon dont en nous parle? Comment ressentons-nous les autres?

Nuestras familias nos enseñan a tratar a otras personas. Te gusta como te trata tu familia? Te gusta como te hablan y las palabras que usan ?
Con las cosas que aprendemos en casa, como usamos nuestras palabras, como hacemos a personas sentir? Las palabras que usamos son importantes ? Hay que elegirlas sabiamente! una vez que las usastes no se pueden devolver .

You may not be happy with someone but there is no need to be mean. Use nice words or no words at all. There is no need to use words that will make them feel bad and you better, no matter what!

Think about it .Have you done that before? To your friends, to your mum, to your teachers to someone you didn't know, to yourself?

Vous n'êtes peut etre pas satisfaite mais il n' a aucune raison d'entre méchants, utilisez de bons mots ou pas des mots du tout.Il n'est pas necesaire d'utiliser des mots qui leur fera du palet vous feras du bien. Peu n'importe quoi.Pensez-y. Avez vous deja dine avant? a vos amis, a votre maman, a vos professeurs qeulqu'n que vous ne connaiassez pas, a vous meme?

Quizá no te estes contento con alguien peor no tienes el derecho de tratarlos mal. usa lindas palabras ninguna palabra . No hay necesidad de usar palabras que va a hacer que esa persona se sienta mal y tu bien, no importa la situación. Pensalo bien has hecho esto antes? A tus amigos, a tu mama, a tus maestros, una persona que no conocias o quizá a tu mismo.

If you see other people using words that are hurtful to you or towards others you can choose to stand up, and say that is wrong. Dont be afraid.

Si tu voyais quelques personne utiliser des mots qui sont fort contre,o qui te fais sentir mal ou fais quelques person . Tu ne dois avoir du peur tus peut choisir disait que ca n'est pas correct .

Tu puedes elegir decir algo, si ves a otra persona usando palabras que te hacen sentir mal o que hacen sentir mal a otros . Tu puedes elegir . No tengas miedo .

Sometimes its the people that love you or you love that are hurtful, your friends your parents . That doesn't mean you need to be too.
Use nice words. Choose wisely.

De temps en Temps les personne que tu aime ou qui t'aime, utilisais des mots qui ne sont pas gentile. ca ne signifie que tu dois faire le meme.
Utilsait de mots gentiles quand tu peut. Choisis sagement

A veces es la gente que te quiere o que tu quieres que dicen cosas que te lastiman, tus amigos, tus padres. Eso no significa que tu debes ser igual. Es difícil. Usa palabras que no lastimen a otros.
Elige sabiamente.

The words you use everyday will make people feel a certain way.

Choose wisely, when words are used often enough people start to believe them . Whether they are nice or not nice!

The not so nice you carry inside you, they swirl around your head . They make you feel sad, its hard to make them go away.

Its hard to believe that they are not true. But words are just words . Choose wisely always.

Les mots que vous utilizes toujours feront ressentira gens une certaine façon.

Choisis sagement, quand les mots sont utilisez assez suivante, le gens le croient. Si les mots sont gentils ou non, ils tourbillonnent autour de ta tete. il vous font sentir triste a l'intérieur. Tu ne peux pas les faire partir.

Il est difficile de penser qu'ils ne sont pas vrais. Les mots ne sont que des mots. Choisis Sagement

La palabras que usamos todos los días hacen que las personas se sientan de alguna forma. Elige sabiamente, cuando las palabras se usan con frecuencia la gente empieza a creerla. Si son buenas o no.

Las pal bras no tan buenas uno los lleva adentro de uno siempre, como remolinos en la cabeza. Te hacen sentir triste y es dicil sacarlos de tu pensamiento.

es didicil creer que no son ciertas . Pero palabras solo son palabras. Elijelas sabiamente.

It doesn't matter where you live, whether you have expensive things or have nothing at all. Whether you live in a family, in a community amongst people that love you.
Words have the same impact on everyone it doesn't matter who you are. So choose wisely.

n'importe pas ou tu habite, ou si tu as des chose chères ou si tu n'avais pas rien. Si tu avais une famille ou si tu vivais dans une communauté qui vous aime.
Mots avais le meme impact. Choisis sagement

No import donde vives si tienes cosas caras o si no tienes nada.
Si vives en una familia, o comunidad que te quiere.

Las palabras tienen el mismo impacto .
Deber elegirlas sabiamente.

So next time you use your words, you choose your words,ask yourself .

Do you see someone who doesn't feel so well and use nice words to make them smile you will smile too. Use nice words anyway just because you can.

Or

Or are you a bully who is sad ?Do you feel bad so you need to use hurtful words to make other people feel bad too and for you to feel better.

Choose your words wisely.

La prochien fois tu utilizes de mot choisis de mot, si tu vois une personne triste utiliser des mots gentile, qui font qu'ils les se sentent bien, qui les font sourire et qui te fais sourire aussi. Utliisez de mots aimables parce que vous pouvais

ou est -ce que vous êtes-vous un tyran qui se sent petit et qui est triste. Est-ce que vos sentez si mal que vous devez utiliser des mots blessants pour que les autres se sentent mal afin que vous vous sentiez mieux.

choisis sagement

La proxima vez que uses tus palabras, eliges tus palabras, preguntate si vez a alguien que no se siente bien utiliza palabras lindas para hacerlos sonreir y tu tambien sonreirás. Usa palabras lindas porque puedes.O sos un tyrano que no esta feliz y tienes que usar palabras que lastiman a otros y te hacen sentir mejor .

Elige tus palabras sabiamente.

Be the person that has the courage to choose words wisely show compassion, respect, empathy and make difference.
Choose to make people smile .
Words are important - Choose wisely -
Together with our words we can change the world.

Tu dois etre la personne une qui a le courage de choisir des mots sagement, pour voi de la compassion, du respect et de l'empathie.
Faire sourire quelq'un.
Des mot son importante- Choisis sagement.
nous souvent changer le monde avec notre mots.

Es importante ser la persona que tiene el coraje de elgir tus palabras sabiamente que muestran, compasión, respeto y empatía.
Elige hacer alguien sonreír.
Palabras son importantes - Elige sabiamente.
Solo con nuestras palabras podemos cambiar el mundo.

Printed in the United States
By Bookmasters